WHAT FLOODS

WHAT FLOODS

AM

RINGWALT

INSIDE THE CASTLE

LAWRENCE, KANSAS

CONTENTS

NOTE FOR
PERFORMANCE

.

Consider this a score. What am I notating? White space, cavernous silence. In your breath, symbols harmonize. In your breath, symbols echo. This is a spell. How does it flood you? Sit in a dark room. Sit in your breath. Walk for hours. Under moon. Under breath-as-room. I'm wearing wormwood perfume, wool sweater. My hair, wet. Under-wear, black. You?

Start with a headache. Let white space dissolve it.

White space—as water. Now, do you hear me?

I'm singing with you. I'm singing with you. The water is warm, and it will become cold. The water is warm, and it will become cold. The water is warm, and it will become cold—slow whorl.

The water is song and I'm singing it through. And when I say *what floods* I mean "what is it that floods" and "what is capable of flooding myself" and "what is capable of flooding someone else" all at once. Someone else: you. In the white space.

An inhalation—

NOTE FOR PERFORMANCE: SUB ROSA

.

There are words that, in order to stay close to my skin, sew themselves stream-thread through pores. Sew themselves in the blank space of breath-between-lips. Sew, so if I bend to the right, living flood. If I bend to the left, dust clinging to the peak of a mountain. And, in a mirror, both hovering above the peak of my skull. Stream-thread loops between past and present. Future, blinding, holds itself in the palm of Collapse. Future, that which is inseminated. Insinuated. All that remains of the breathing-be is a stream. All that remains is my *be*. I don't need you to know what I mean. I need you to feel my stream-thread reach.

WHAT
FLOODS

what floods
            when loose-
            limbed i
dis-
    tend?

                                        (softly)

soft-
      ly—

              soft-
ly—i tend

 lucid
     i
blow blue

lurid i
        comb through

                        these
stream-threads

                         (do i
know you?)

you comb
sand

                                        (slowly)

slow-
        ly—

             you
make land

with burning
bark

with dove's
beak

            my tongue
sweet
so

                                        (softly)

            soft-
ly—

soft—

6

       this lily
wilt

     lily-
willed in
slow clean

                                  (slowly)

my spine
bare

what floods
then

what floods
then

what slow-soft
slow-soft

distance

A song I want to sing so dearly: "I See Thee Better in the Dark" by Josephine Foster. No lyrics to find online. I contemplated transcribing, but her words self-veil as voice progresses. A kind of articulated darkness. I'm on the *Memory and Trauma* Wikipedia page: "Memory is ascribed by psychology as the ability of an organism to store, retain, and subsequently retrieve information." Why do I feel the need to cry?

Now, I'm on the *Effects of Stress and Memory* Wikipedia page. Wikipedia is safer tonight. Another search result took me to an article saying people with PTSD "over-remember" an event, a trauma, making it worse than it actually was. This page says, instead: "The effects of stress on memory include interference with person's capacity to encode memory and the ability to retrieve information." What I am capable of. What I enfold. Still, retrieval is mostly out of the question. I flood. I flow.

Memory. "It is between séances." That's Theresa Hak Kyung Cha.

"Memory trespasses our limits." That's Etel Adnan.

Still. Tell me: where did my blood go? Where—

> I see thee
> better in
> the dark
>
> I see thee
> better in
> the dark
>
> *(I think I see*
> *a knight*
> *I'm gonna*
> *fuck him*
> *for a while)*

"The Hope Only of Empty Men." That's Anna von Hausswolff's voice through organ pipes. That's a pearlescent sun on the horizon, dripping semen. That's a trance I submit to. That's a trance, trespassing. That's the *between.* The sun and secretion. The sun and its secret. The son and my weeping. I see thee better / in séance-intermission. I see *me* in / memory-remission. In a pearlescent sun wrung through organ pipes. I think I see the night. I can see for miles. I can see the limit, the mountain-blade.

I can see what floods.

Every time a sound returns, I feel it press against my exhalation. I have to take it in or let it live upon my breath. As, on a walk in early summer, I hear a dog bark at its own echo—down the hill, to the waterfront, and back again.

What echoes is, necessarily, a repetition. It follows: what repeats is an echo. Porous accumulation. Porous pulse.

Every time you say my name, I am transformed. My hair grows longer. Shoulder blades, soften. Every time you say my name, my tongue curls back. Less than a centimeter at a time. Still, I know nothing of control.

Every time the vowel *a*. Every time the hymnal page.

"That's the place where later on, once the present is left behind, I must stay to the exclusion of everywhere else." That's Marguerite Duras.

To echo, to trigger. Finger to a blade.

Magnolia flower blooming in my brain.

"As soon as I perceive it, as soon as I name it, the sublime triggers—it has always already triggered." That's Julia Kristeva.

And: "There are seconds—they come five or six at a time—when you suddenly feel the presence of eternal harmony in all its fullness. It is nothing earthly. I don't mean that it is heavenly, but a man in his earthly semblance can't endure it. He has to undergo a physical change or die."

Less than a centimeter at a time.

It's not enough. Limbs to be raised.

Earth to be razed.

Here is a dog at the top of a hill. The dog—genderless, only sound, only sounding—barks. There, at the bottom of the hill, the dog's voice re-sounds, re-turns, re-routes up the hill. Constellates out. Here, the dog replies. In the constellation. The landscape isn't important, but it makes the sound.

Kant calls the sublime an agitation, that of "rapid alternation."

(Who are you, who sound just like me?)

"And this emotion is a vibration." That's Catherine Clément.

And this motion. Every time the vowel *a*. Every time the hymnal—say.

In June, Will and I drive through Kentucky. I note the magnolias. Say: after everything, I hope I'm something like a magnolia tree. So many years old. So tall. So saturated, feminine-fragrant. Let my spine—like the trunk of a magnolia tree. Let my speech—sweet as petal, edged as bark.

Who are you, who sound just like me? I must change or die.

Repulsion and attraction. Pressing to my breath.

I was with my dog in the lake, once. I was with my dog in the grass. I pressed my cheek to the earth. I whispered, so as not to echo. I whispered: "to go backward and inward simultaneously." That's Cecilia Vicuña.

I read *Syncope*. I walk beside the river with Will. I remember—Clément quotes Bataille: "a being can only be touched where it yields." I can't get through to Will. He's in the dark. He says he's scared to see himself clearly.

But a being can only *be*.

Let my speech—sweet as wood-groove, edged as flower.

Let—agitation. Transformation. Every night, the same tear.

Down the hill of my face.

Now, I'm in the daylight. Where I yield.

I walk beside the river. I round a corner, climb a residential street. From farther up the hill, an elderly woman waves to me. From the window of the Milton Home. The woman looks right at me—as if she knows me, as if she's seen me before. I wave back, grinning. For five minutes, she waves. She stops. Again. She waves. Delight and dementia. Sublime recognition. Her hand moving up and down in the air.

"It's you," she could have said. And then, forgot.

And then—*who are you, who sound just like me?*

It's Dickinson, after all.

> I see thee better in the dark,
> I do not need a light.
> The love of thee a prism be
> Excelling violet.
>
> I see thee better for the years   5
> That hunch themselves between,
> The miner's lamp sufficient be
> To nullify the mine.
>
> And in the grave I see thee best—
> Its little panels be   10
> A-glow, all ruddy with the light
> I held so high for thee!
>
> What need of day to those whose dark
> Hath so surpassing sun,
> It seem it be continually   15
> At the meridian?

How a song can hold language. Poem transposed.
How a song can hold language. My mouth *(softly)* O—

As a child, I walked along the road in Michigan. Singing to myself.

(What song? Memory bends. *That hunch themselves between.*)

Now, I sing while I sweat. I sing for the dead. I sing from my bed. A friend texts me "For All" by Amen Dunes. Says it sounds like me. I listen on repeat for an hour. The singer's voice, then others. Repetition—meditation over blade. The singer's voice, then others. Making a blanket. Making a shroud.

All these visions I can see quite plain.

And then—does he sing, *stand amongst the doily field?* The *doting field?*

I want to lie in this *field*—dark, un-nameable—and feel the ground hold me. I want to lie in this *field*—dark, un-nameable—and stay for days. Multiplicity of séance. Prism in mountain-blade, split-stream. How my eyes will drift, see double, more. And elsewhere.

I sing to my memory: *If it's dark, go home. I won't be there.*

But I'll comb for years.

I saw Amen Dunes perform in Cambridge when I was eighteen. Took the train from Boston. Took the sound of metal underground. The street, humming, above. I had no clue to comb. Simultaneity of experience. Had no clue to—memory, hunching states away.

And I performed a kind of sleep that night—too much to drink. And I met my best friend that night. We danced on top of a table, unbuttoned our shirts. We hugged like sisters and swayed our hips. I remember arching my back, looking up to the ceiling. Hours could have passed. Days. It wasn't dancing music. It was articulated dark.

To nullify the mine, or—

I see thee better, or—

go home. I won't be there.

And I have a song, inside a river.
And I have a song. I named it "River"—

I wrote a poem about Edith Piaf when I was twenty, after my first flashback. My professor at the time asked me if I knew her biography, but I only knew her song. Now, I'm on the *Edith Piaf* Wikipedia page:

> Piaf's mother abandoned her at birth, and she lived for a short time with her maternal grandmother, Emma (Aïcha). When her father enlisted with the French Army in 1916 to fight in World War I, he took her to his mother, who ran a brothel in Bernay, Normandy. There, prostitutes helped look after Piaf. The bordello had two floors and seven rooms, and the prostitutes were not very numerous, "about ten poor girls" as she later described, in fact five or six were permanent and a dozen for market and any busy days. The sub-mistress of the brothel, "Madam Gaby" could be considered a little like family since she became godmother of Denise Gassion, the half-sister born in 1931. Edith believed her weakness for men came from mixing with prostitutes in her grandmother's brothel.

I thought that when a boy called a girl, the girl would never refuse, she said.

And I have a song inside a river.
And I have a song named "River"—

and flooded through, still I will
sing—my love.

and my love wasn't one of refusal
my love was one of wet roses

and my love wasn't one of magnolia
my love was one of damp music

(slowly)

and i was a well, inverting
in mountain-blade

my body was
sleeping

under a spell
from that

first blow

and my body was a site
for invasion

my body was home,
incapacitation

unnamed, another kind of horror—
again, again

(slowly)

and i was a comb, reverting—

wet rose, magnolia,
cold candle-flame

slow-soft slow-soft
i was a comb,

rewiring—

i dreamed dark,
spine bare

my body my love
i climbed

softly through
stream-threads

my body my love
i climbed

up mountain-
blade to music

To hold a feeling in my mind and not to write it down.

•

I stand under the showerhead, washed in sound,
and claim this gut as mine—

                              And water

on my forehead in a stream.

And

                                        water on my forehead
                                        in a stream.

And—always—this horizontal leaning. This sleep steeping.
Slow bleeding.

•

When I sigh, I am breathing.
When I sigh, I am leaning. That place I go
in sleep—
                              again,
                  again.

Where dirt road. Where tree swell.
Where crystal bloom. Where water.

Where—
incomprehensible height of hills.

Where—
I dance on a stage, either bleeding
or leaning. Find light
under refracted candle
flames. My body—
candle-blade.

And water on my forehead in a stream.

•

Where the caves flood with water and I float out.

When the caves flood with water, I float out.

When the flood. When the flo—

•

What does it feel like to be in the stream.
What does it feel like to be held, palms on my skull.
What does it feel like to feel. Palms on my skull.
What does it feel like to hold.

When I sigh, I am breathing. That place I go to bleed.
When I sigh, I am palms; leaves, leaving—

•

                              and crystal bloom.

And Mon Dieu. Water on my forehead in a stream. And
     palm-leaves
on my palms, cutting into crease. When I breathe. Washed
     in sound.

Whose voice—deep, soil-dark, I take in. Whose voice—
to bleed against vein, which is to embrace.

And water from my mouth.

And—*do you like the feeling of the mud?*

Let a crystal break. In soil. Let a break refract. In holy oil. Quartz, mud, my body on the ground. Not buried. Not carried. Ophelia in worm-light. Me, spinning. In magnifying worn-light. Me, singing. *Mon dieu, mon dieu, mon dieu.* From a voice, near-imperceptible, inside a stream. Inside a bleed. When I sigh, I am palms—leaves leaving. Palms—skin, cleaving.

what floods
(whorl)

what floods
(whole)

what floods
(heart)

what floods
(dark)

what floods
(world)

what floods
(room)

•

whorl floods
what?

there is a ruby
in your drool,
in your mouth

some room. i hold it
in my palms
and blow

keep it beating

keep it bleeding
like a heart, ruby

in the pool

in the whorl
if you ask
me it be-

comes a heart

•

ruby in the dark

world floods
what?

listening to "lucette stranded on the island"
        in my car

the leaves, ruby
in blood-whorl
road scene blur

•

listening to "lucette stranded on the island"
        in the shower

i don't remember much but

water on my shoulders

it's the bells i like
repeated piano note

it's the bells, voice moving

                                        (slowly)

how it wants

there's a ruby in your song
when you speak it eases up
your throat

(slowly)
(slowly)

give it to me

In January 2017, I started EMDR therapy. Now, I'm on the *Eye movement desensitization and reprocessing* Wikipedia page.

The second paragraph, a single line: "The way it might work is uncertain."

To get to my therapist's office, I had to take the green line to Park, the red line to Harvard, and then the 74 bus to Belmont. There, I learned that EMDR mimics REM sleep: the crucial point of present-time for trauma to be processed.

In Belmont, I learned about neuroplasticity.

From Wikipedia: "EMDR therapy was first developed by Francine Shapiro upon noticing that certain eye movements reduced the intensity of disturbing thought."

A horizontal strip of light was placed in front of me, balanced on a tripod. This strip, nearly six feet long, emitted what's called a bilateral stimulation. From the right and then to the left, a dot of light moved back and forth. I chose the speed: slow, like breath. A vibrating pod was placed under my right thumb, which buzzed in sync with the light.

This movement echoed sleep.

(Who are you, who sound just like me?)

Kant calls the sublime an agitation, that of "rapid alternation."

"And this emotion is a vibration." That's Catherine Clément.

And this motion. Every time the vowel *a*. Every time the hymnal—

Memory. "It is between séances." That's Theresa Hak Kyung Cha.

I recalled violence.

My therapist asked me to envision a place I could store the memories. I needed somewhere to reprocess them into. I chose Lake Michigan. Combed before water.

Lake Michigan, a sieve. I poured out from my mind: his tongue, his overdoses, my body bent backward. I poured out from my mind: *I'm gonna fuck you up.* Poured out: hands on my abdomen, blackout in snow. Honey-blood, bruised legs, the clothes I left behind.

What was caught in the lake-sieve
poured back into my hands:

my self, in present-time,
shedding dead weight. My self—

keep it beating
like a heart

with water-skin,
palms humming.

And she asked me: what does it feel like to be in the stream?

What does it feel like to *be*?

What floods, what   *(slowly)*

        floors me?

Sun through   the window,

white fire   through hair.

I want to sing.   Have it touch

someone. Please,   let me sing.

In a clearing,   in still water,

your palms   on my skull.

In a clearing,   in still water,

I cut a flower   from hell.

Let me sing,   let me bleed

where wings   would be.

Let me sing,   water through

teeth, while   my cat

cleans   her coat

of dove bones   and deer blood

and lilies.   Let me sing

water through   what floods.

(What floods?)

She rests on

when I wake,

There is something

being to yield.

O,

I was delirious

my chest

says *listen.*

to learn here,

O,

O—

until sleep.

"Elektra," Lee Noble, *The Hell of You Come In.*
"Miracle," Cocorosie, *The Adventures of Ghosthorse & Stillboy.*
"Garlands," Sarah Davachi, *Let Night Come on Bells End the Day.*
"Malorum Sanatio," Alice Notley, if read by Marianne Faithfull.
"Malorum Sanatio," Alice Notley, if read by Mahalia Jackson.
"Malorum Sanatio," Alice Notley, if read by both at once.

(slowly)

I need this pace.
I need to sing—

plum-soft, quartz
in the stream.

Handful of grass
from a stranger's

lawn. The sleeve
of a grey sweater

singed by flame.
Your opening mouth.

(Who
are you,

who sound
just like me?)

Self-echo.
Self-echo.

In the curve
of a trigger-bed,

which is mountain-
blade. I pulse

in the air
like a spirit.

Held out—
by who?

That crystal
hovering

in the air. Right
in front of me.

That blood-purple
carrot held out

before horse.
That quivering

bird held
before panther.

(By who?)

And—the faces are here.

And we all speak cold, cold water.

And we all sing, here—cold, cold water.

And—sand rolling off a cliff by breaths of wind.

Sand rolling of a cliff by breaths of wind. Breaths from un-
real lungs, so big. To be empty-headed, clear-handed. The
faces are breathing. No time to be between. My hands have
skin, after all. My hands can sweat and bleed. Can pool. Can
hold out, which is to offer—something was telling me to go.
Something was telling me—let the longest sigh. Self-echo.
In the curve of trigger-bed.

I'm building a comb out of water. I'm building a home.

The landscape isn't important, but it makes the sound.

What do I need to say? The first time I expressed love it was through Facebook chat. I said it to a violence across the country. I wept even then. How he cut me. I was listening to "Mon Dieu" by Edith Piaf at the time. Somehow, the fact of that first blow hasn't changed my reaction to the song. Somehow, despite—severed tongue, bruised legs, blackout in snow—it floods me like blood, like saliva-slick, like magnolia pulp. The horror of continuation, mutation. The song floods me—like smoke from a censer in a pitch-black room. I write to the same song on repeat. I writhe to the same song on repeat. Do I write the same song? I want this space to be an invitation. Out of my interior and into yours.

I see thee better in the dark, I do not need a light.

Take a picture of yourself on the floor and send it to me. Or, take a picture of yourself on the floor and place it here—on this page. I especially want to see the woman from the Milton Home. Here, one more time.

Here. *It's you.*

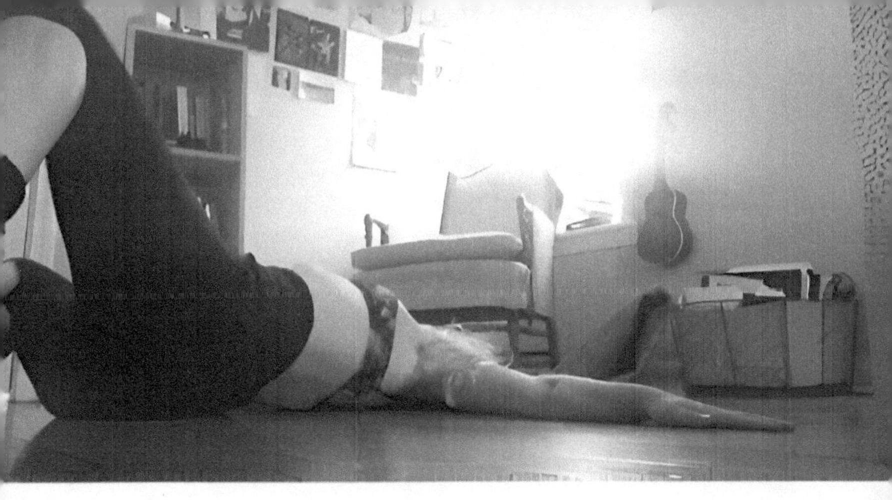

mon dieu, mon dieu, mon dieu...
laissez-le-moi
encore un peu
mon amoureux

un jour, deux jours, huit jours...
laissez-le-moi
encore un peu
à moi...

le temps de s'adorer,
de se le dire,
le temps de se fabriquer
des souvenirs

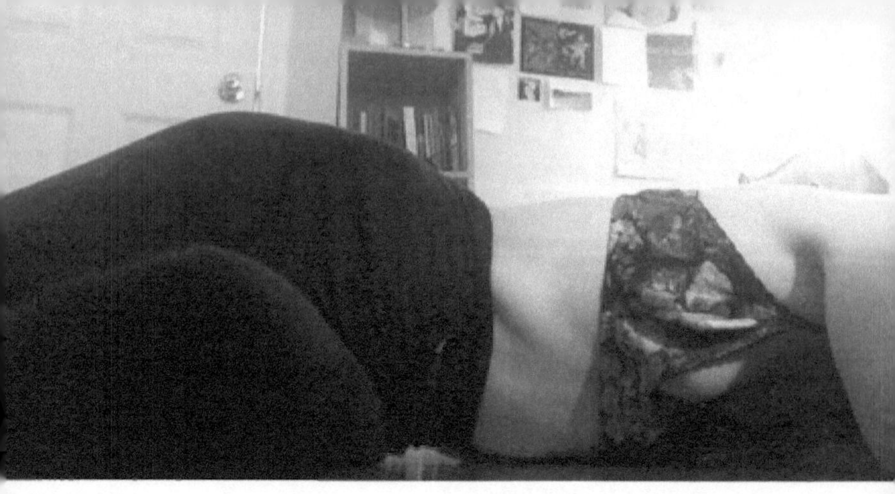

mon dieu, oh oui...mon dieu
laissez -le-moi
remplir un peu
ma vie...

mon dieu, mon dieu, mon dieu...
laissez-le-moi
encore un peu,
mon amoureux

six mois, trois mois, deux mois...
laissez-le-moi
pour seulement
un mois...

le temps de commencer
ou de finir,
le temps d'illuminer
ou de souffrir

mon dieu, mon dieu,
mon dieu!

même si j'ai tort,
laissez-le moi
un peu...
meme si j'ai tort,
laissez-le-moi
encore...

o

o

o

i was delirious

until sleep